MW00984948

LOVING THOUGHTS
for
Increasing Prosperity

Louise L. Hay

Hay House
Carson, California

Library of Congress Cataloging-in-Publication Data

Hay, Louise L.
    Loving thoughts for increasing prosperity / Louise L. Hay.
        p.   cm.
    ISBN 1-56170-068-1 : $5.95
    1. Success--Psychological aspects. 2. Affirmations. I. Title.
BF637.S8H34   1993
158'.12--dc20   93-13180
                                                          CIP

Design & Typesetting by: Michele Lanci-Altomare

93 94 95 96 97 98   10 9 8 7 6 5 4 3 2 1
First Printing, September 1993

Published and Distributed in the United States by:
Hay House, Inc.
P.O. Box 6204
Carson, CA 90749-6204

Printed in the United States of America
on Recycled Paper

INTRODUCTION

The power of positive thinking is a well-known healing force even within the medical community. The positive, loving thoughts on the following pages are nothing more than positive affirmations.

You may feel that thinking a positive thought cannot possibly change your life, but how many times have you repeatedly affirmed a negative thought about yourself until finally it became true for you? Why not change those negative thoughts to positive ones?

I like to compare positive affirmations to planting a seed. You don't just plant the seed and get a beautiful flower the next day. It takes time. First you must water and nurture the seed and make sure it is safe from harm. It is the same with positive affirmations. You may not see changes immediately, but with enough nurturing and encouragement you can change your old negative way of thinking and look at things in a new and positive light.

Use these affirmations daily and over time you will begin to see your life turn in new direction and you will reap a bountiful harvest of positive, loving endeavors for yourself.

All is well,

Louise L. Way

Today...

I choose to attract prosperity.

Today...

I accept a life filled with rewards and fulfillment.

Today...

*everything I touch
is a success.*

Today...

I know how to accept gifts graciously with a simple "thank you."

Today...

*I create a good life
for myself
because I deserve.*

Today...

*I allow prosperity
to enter my life
on a new level.*

Today...

*I rejoice
in life's abundance
and appreciate
all that I have.*

Today...

*I trust life
to supply me
with everything I need.*

Today...

*unexpected good
is coming my way from
unexpected sources.*

Today...

*all my needs
and desires are met
before I even ask.*

Today...

I allow my income to constantly expand.

Today...

*I allow myself
to receive abundance
from the Ocean of Life.*

Today...

life knows my needs
and generously
supplies them all.

Today...

*it is my birthright
to share in the
abundance and
prosperity of this world.*

Today...

*I am unlimited
in my wealth.*

Today...

*I am open
and receptive
to new avenues
of income.*

Today...

*my good comes from
everywhere
and everyone
and everything.*

Today...

I give myself
permission to be
all that I can be
and to deserve
the very best in life.

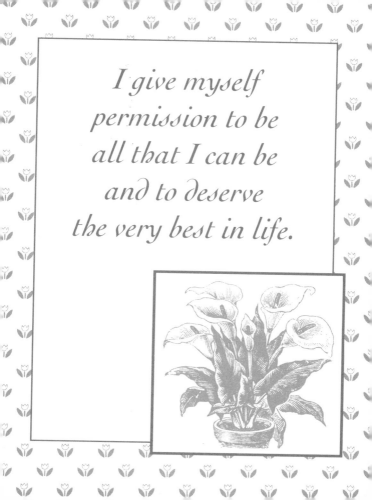

Today...

I am totally and completely supported by the Universe.

Today...

*I accept with joy
and pleasure all
the good life offers me.*

Today...

my prosperous thoughts
create my
prosperous world.

Today...

I release all belief in lack and limitation.

Today...

begins a new era
of prosperity
and security.

Today...

*I give
myself permission
to prosper.*

Today...

*I bless my bills
with love
and pay them
with joy.*

Today...

*I am safe
and secure
and financially
solvent.*

Today...

*I give thanks
for all good and
all supply.*

Today...

*new doors
are opening.*

Today...

*my life is filled
with an abundance
of all good.*

Today...

*all is well
in my
prosperous world.*

BOOKS IN THIS SERIES

Loving Thoughts for a Perfect Day
Loving Thoughts for Health and Healing
Loving Thoughts for Increasing Prosperity
Loving Thoughts for Loving Yourself

For a free catalog, call
1-800-654-5126

HAY
HOUSE